THE JENNIFER JOURNAL

- Or -

A Father's Reminiscences

William Linden

Foreword

Jen, this book is about you and for you. You may wish to share it with your children if you eventually have any, or with anyone else you choose. It is my personal gift to you — a giveback for all the priceless and sometimes utterly remarkable memories you've given me and Mom, by being you. I'm starting to laugh now thinking of some of them. I'll hold it.

I also address a general reader sometimes, using the old-fashioned term, "gentle reader", because I want people to know that if they don't record their children's memorable moments they will forget them. Not "may," will. They, people, will object saying that, "If someone said to me, 'Remember when ... ' I'd surely remember those moments." But they will not. Not all of them. Not fully and truly remember —especially the full backstory. The story is critical.

Enjoy.

The Jennifer Journal

- or -

A Father Remembers

I was there at the crowning. Not of Queen Elizabeth II, but at your birth.

Mom was very tired, and the doctors were considering whether to do a caesarian. Mom urgently asked me, "Do you see anything?" I said, "I think so." So, she summoned up her reserves and gave two extra mighty pushes and out, "into the light," you slid.

Now, ... you didn't cry! You seemed to just look. You just looked. And I thought, "if she is capable of thinking anything, it would be something like, 'I can handle this.'"
I know infants' eyes don't coordinate and focus until weeks later, and that at birth newborns don't 'think,' but there we were....

I couldn't believe you weren't crying. I counted my breaths because I knew if I didn't have some external measure, I would have a hard time believing *myself*, let alone have anyone else believe me. Even now. But I know it to be true because I counted my own breaths. "Isn't she going to cry? Don't all babies cry?" Seven breaths.

I don't know if the nurse holding you tapped your back —I didn't see her swat you— but, finally, you cried. '…Okay, everything's normal.'

Later, someone, meaning to impart something to me said, "She's an Old Soul." I didn't know what that meant, I still don't, but I suppose it means, 'Someone who's been around, who looks at things with a balanced eye, who isn't tipped toward frantic.' And, that is true. Maybe a decade later the mother of one of your friend's said, "She's the Voice of Reason." Her daughter certainly was not, and that may have given added reason why she so appreciated you, but regardless, you have proved that opinion to be true.

So, this journal is an advisory to all parents who think that they will surely remember everything memorable. **Not!**

I used to think like that too and I was wrong. Having you in my mid-fifties, I knew better than to credit myself like that. And really, just as important, and in many cases *more* important, a picture is not enough. The backstory often makes the moment.

The thousand words makes the picture, not the other way around, not the snapshot. The photo doesn't tell the story. *I had even forgot some of these memories even though I had written them down over the years!*

This is an anthology of my most memorable recollections of you; written down, fortunately. Thank you for them. They are a gas!

Going forward, readers, I will use initials: J for Jennifer, K for Karen, her mom, and W for William, me.

Contents

1 Outthink Her?

2 God, Pee-pee and Matches

3 The King of Sleepyland (*Re di Sleepilandia*)

4 Honeybells

5 Are you *Kidding* me?

6 Me Do!

7 A Guardian Lion and The *Marseilles*

8 *O Tannenbaum* (*Oh Christmas Tree*)

9 How Do Bones Work?

10 A Present for Father

11 The Concept of a Good Death

12 First Italian Words

13 You'll Be Canceled!

14 Different Driving Styles

15 Wherefore Babies?

16 Playing Teacher

17 I Am Six!

18 Thanks, but....

19 Men

20 Go On! It's Fascinating!

21 A Gift For Father

22 Languages

23 Italian

24 A Future Epistemologist?

25 Put Out Who?!

26 Santa

27 Generosity

28 Intuitive Economics

29 Emotional Fact-checking

30 The Downside of Human Nature

31 Yeah, Sure....

32 The Cat Who Converses

33 He's Just a Psychologist!

34 A Good Question ... and ... An Answer

35 Mom's Dream: Jennifer's Baby

36 What can I Leave Her?

37 Hole Smoke! What Questions!

38 The Cougar Dream

39 Ba Duan Jen

40 Haiku

41 Another "Me Do!" Story

42 Why Aren't My Half-Brothers in My Life?

1   Outthink Her?

It's evening, after dinner. Karen, Jennifer and I are on a walk around the condo complex. You are on your tricycle. We're on our way back.

Karen asks me something. I answer. She responds. Adult talk. Jennifer slows the trike and asks something to understand what we were talking about, which we did not want her to be part of. We always try not to exclude her, but there are boundaries. We're stymied, and time is ticking.

I see that Karen can't come up with how to field this one, so I take centerstage. I say something, and go on a bit, and Jen says something, the atmosphere relaxes and Jennifer motors on. The distractor worked.

Karen looks at me very distinctly. I look at her and try to put words on the effect that her look has on me. A few steps later I say, "I think I know what you were just thinking."

K: Go ahead.

W: Is this the last time that he or I will be able to get around Jennifer?

K: Yes!

God, Pee-pee and Matches

(Jennifer: 3 years, 10 months) Background. Karen is at work; night shift hospital nurse at this point. Jennifer in bed with me, having a somewhat hard time going off to sleep. After about five minutes of silence, this....)

J: Dadda.

W: Yes, Jen.

J: What does 'god' mean?

W: (!!!) God, ... god... Uhm, 'god' is a word. God is a word people use when they don't know what else to say. And they're either very happy or sad.

J: But what is 'god?'

W: Jen, I don't believe there anything called god. It's just a sound, a word people use to express feelings.

(brief silence)

J: What about baby Jesus? [Her religioused-up cousins must have talked with her when we were not there.]

W: Baby Jesus grew up to be Jesus. Mr. Jesus. If we were close relatives, you'd call him Uncle Jesus. Like Uncle Dennis or

Uncle Paul. He was a man and if he had had a daughter, she would have called him, Dadda. Not Mr. God, Dadda.

J: Oh. (uncertain)

W: He was a good man, a teacher —and what made him good?— because he taught people to treat each other better.

J: Was he god?

W: No, he was a man. A good man. And there were many others, too. One called Buddha. But they were not god.

(silence)

(some minutes later)

J: Dadda?

W: Yes?

J: You know my tootie looks like this? (gestures with hands)

W: Yes.

J: But where does the pee-pee really come from?

W: (!) Well, Jen, let's agree your tootie looks like this (I mirror her gesture with hands). Well, inside here, there's a hole and that's where the pee-pee really comes from.

J: Oh.

(silence)

J: Dadda?

W: Yes, …. Jennifer.

J: How does the lamp work?

W: Well Jen honey, I can't fully explain it to you, but it's something like this (and I bring it down to…) if we push the button it closes a circuit and energy runs around and that makes the bulb give off light.

(silence)

J: Dadda?

W: Yes, Jennifer, what is it?

J: One more question.

W: No. I gave you three. Now put yourself to sleep.

J: No, seriously. Just one more.

W: (knowing it is a losing battle) … OK, Last one. What is it?

J: Dadda, how does a match work?

(She had seen me light and tend a fire twice that week)

W: (I explain.)

(silence)

{What great questions! Jennifer, 4-and-a-half-years)

3   The King of Sleepyland (aka / Il re di sleepilandia)

We five —grandma, grandpa and we three— are on vacation for nine days, heading first to Vermont and then to Lake Skaneateles and the New York State Fair. We're in grandpa's large Lincoln.

We've been in the car for an hour or two since the pit stop. The adults know we have about two hours to go before reaching the motel. A good time to nap. An especially good time for a child to nap.

Now, ("gentle reader,") you have to know that when putting Jen to sleep I would sometimes, as an aid to relaxing her, tell her that the King of Sleepyland (always referred to in Italian, the *re di sleepilandia*), flies by and when he touches the roof of a house, all who are in it feel tired, very tired, and they go off to Sleepylandia.

So, I start the patter:

W: Oh, Jennifer, I think I just felt the *re di sleepilandia* touch the car with his …

J: Oh yeah? The *Re di Sleepilandia* is in New Jersey!

We can't believe it! The four adults. Flabbergasted. Grandpa cracks up! And the rest of us are so astonished that our jaws drop.

{Not yet 5 and declaring in effect that the *Re* has no jurisdiction where we are! Or maybe just, "Don't hand me that!" But done on the fly, with total confidence.}

On the return ride from Vermont to Skaneateles, New York, it was a bit tiring. So, we invented a game. Who am I thinking of?

W: Do you want to go first, Jen?

J: No. You go.

W: OK. He's got a fun personality. He's got big, beautiful brown eyes. He's …

J: I know. I know. James!

W: Right. Good. OK, who goes now?

J: I'll go. My turn!

W: OK, go.

J: She's a girl. And she's very nice, most of the time. She has pretty blue eyes and she sometimes doesn't listen to her parents.

Four adults are stumped. I'm thinking, Who would she be speaking about almost critically? Claire, no. Greta, no. Emma, no, and she has brown eyes? All four adults are still silent.

J: Do you know?

None of us comes forward.

J: Guess!

One by one, 'I don't know,' we all confess.

J: It's me!

Oh-my-god looks! All around! We were genuinely stumped. What really knocked our socks off was her capacity to objectify herself and sustain it for the whole turn.

(Jennifer: 4 years, 11 months)

Honeybells

Your Mom, (Karen,) is in the kitchen eating a honeybell. It is so delicious she invites me to share it, which I do. It is so good that she says, "I'm gonna have me another!" You walk in.

J What's that Mommy?

K: A honeybell.

W: They're too good for children.

J: Oh, they're *not* too good for children. I just don't *want* a honeybell!

{5 years, 4months!}

5   Are You Kidding Me?

(I have to go back a bit now. In approximately December 2001, Grandpa Frank had a stroke and in February 2002 he lived with us for a month because the rehabilitation center is not far from us and quite far from where Grandma lives. You were three years old.)

So, one Sunday morning you and grandpa were having waffles for a treat. You ate, Grandpa was eating, and I was in the kitchen waiting for my rye toast to pop up. You turned from looking out the back door window and asked,

J: Can I have more waffles?

W: We've finished it all, Jen. There is no more.

J: But I want some more.

I repeated what I said. You said, 'I want some more waffles.'

(So, taking a different tack, I say in a very nice, teacher-ish voice)

Oh, Jen, did you know that bread and waffles are actually made from the same thing?

You wheeled around and said, 'Are you *kidding* me!'

Grandpa guffawed so hard I thought he might go into a choking spasm.

I couldn't believe it. When I walked into the dining area and Grandpa and I looked at each other, I shrugged and shook my head, and he almost went into another laughing fit.

When he was calm, I said, 'Yep, that's how she is.' And he chuckled again.

6   Me Do!

    To further document the previous story, I don't know how many times at two, two-and-a-half and three, you would say, "No. Me do!"

    For instance, to help you off with your shoes, which at that age you shouldn't have been able to do —to pull the lace string through and loosen the top crossed laces and wiggle your foot out of the shoe— but you did. Repeatedly.

    In fact, one day, when I had forgotten your competence, you flung my hand off your shoe and said, "Me do!"

7 A Guardian Lion, and *The Marseilles*

We were in Paris for the wedding of Aunt Shelley's son, Nick, and Elise Moscoso. You were exactly three. We know that because it was mid-September and your birthday is on the 17th. (By the way, the weather was absolutely perfect for all seven days, a coincidence that does not happen often, I was informed.)

Anyway, there are a lot of pigeons in Paris, as there are in many big cities, and you had seen "The Lion King" video and "The Lion King II" many times. You liked the character, Poomba, a sweet-hearted wild pig who at one point charges into a flock of vultures, to disperse them, to save Simba, (I think). Anyway again, we had to watch you carefully to restrain you from continuously taking off after the pigeons (and maybe following them into the street).

Well, one day we were in the Luxembourg Gardens, (a very large park). There were hundreds of pigeons. You were in heaven. You lit out after them shouting, "Here comes Poomba!" And you delighted in sending columns of pigeons into the air.

Next, we had rented an apartment in Paris. It was OK. Karen thought it was "charming." It was OK.

One night you had a bad dream. You told us that there were bad ants who were biting you on the leg and your stuffed animal, a lion, Coco, took the ants off you and threw them to the ground!

OK, but when we were getting dressed that morning, Mom noticed that you had red marks on your legs.

It would be really nice to have a guardian lion to protect us during sleep.

The above is just part of the backstory that could never be captured by a photo.

In the spring of '02, Shelley told us that Nick was engaged and that the wedding would be in Paris, in September, the following year. Here's the main story.

So, I launched on a campaign to teach you the French national anthem, *The Marseilles*. Now, (gentle reader), you must exert your imagination to estimate *how* much enthusiasm, and trickery, and persistence, was involved in a pursuit of this sort! Getting a two-and-a-half-year-old to feel like singing, in a foreign language. *And*, trying to prime her to anticipate what a hoot it would be if the people who we would be with would hear a diminutive American singing their song?

Scene: The wedding reception at the Moscoso's apartment (in Montmarte). When it was over, finally, from your point of view, and you declined a stupid idea from your father. You know what it was. What would any self-respecting two-and-a-half-year-old do but refuse? You are not a wind-up toy that performs when wound. Of course not!

One other fact must be mentioned. The staircase of the Moscoso's building is quite wide, in a grand European way. It had very nice wrought ironwork and marble stairs.

So, it was time to say final, final, final adieus and we were leaving the Moscoso's, having said all our goodbyes and done all our kisses times two. Mr. Moscoso escorted us to the door, with his Gitane in his lips and bidding us goodbye again. We start down the stairs, me leading, you next and Karen at the rear. It was our last chance!

Literally, it was the moment of no return. I start to sing the M. The stairway was like an acoustic amplifier. It must have been that that captured you, because all of a sudden, I hear in back of me, a chorus of one, joining me to make the music louder! Cacophonous! And that *further* stimulated you! So, we marched down the grand staircase stomping to the amplified *Marseilles*.

Mr. Moscoso could not believe his ears! It was so loud and he was so happy and he heard how happy you were, that after a few lines, *he* joined in! So the first two Lindens marched triumphantly down the stairs while up on top was Mr. Moscoso airing away, "*aux armes citoyens! formez vos bataillons!*" etc., all of it *roaring* off the stairs and walls, Moscoso *laughing* in jags, in between his coughing fits. Laughing delightedly, not believing it, and coughing.

Yes!!! A year's work not wasted!

9 _O Tannenbaum_ (*Oh Christmas Tree*)

It's Open-school night. Your kindergarten teacher, Mrs. P, is talking with us about you. (I'm thinking, Yeah, yeah, that's all fine and well, but that's surface; you're not seeing her. Her individuality. Or at least you're not saying anything that suggests that you do.)

I ask Mrs. P, who had recently been to Germany to visit her husband who was in the military, "You know, Jennifer likes to sing. Do you sing in class?" Mrs. P: "Oh, yes."

But nothing more forthcoming. I suggest to her that the class, Jennifer and she, could have fun hearing Christmas songs sung in a different language.

A polite nod-smile. Nothing. (She has a nice personality but for a responsive mind, a bag of prunes.) I say, "Mrs. P, you probably don't know it, but Jennifer can sing songs in several languages, other than English."

(She really doesn't get it. She doesn't ask. So, I have to spoon-feed her.)

"You know, maybe, from being in Germany recently, if you know, *Oh Tannenbaum,* you and Jennifer could sing it to the class, as part of Fun Time."

(OK. Maybe. Who knows what her reaction really was.)

Nevertheless!, a few weeks later, Jennifer told Karen and me, that she and Mrs. P went next door to Mrs. F's class and sung, *O Tannenbaum* to them! *Auf Deutsch*! (In German.)

I love that. At age 5 you had the confidence to sing, in front of a class, in a foreign language yet. I hope you always have your Voice.

10   How Do Bones Work?

(Approximately 8PM. Back home. We had driven Karen to work at the hospital for her 7P to 7A shift.)

J: (on the pot) Dadda?

W; Yes...

J: Come in here. I want to ask you something.

W: Why don't you enjoy what you're doing, and then when you finish, you'll ask me?

J: No. I want to ask now!

W: OK.

J: How do bones work? (Gestures with her leg and arm.)

W: Do you mean, How do they work, or how do they grow?

J: How they work. Like this. (She gestures again.)

W: Well, inside our skin we have flesh and muscles and bones and nerves. And tendons, that are like strings. When we want to move and arm or leg, our brain sends a signal down a nerve and the nerve makes the muscle move, expand or contract, and the tendon and muscle pulls the bone. That way the whole leg, or arm, or finger moves. ... Okay?

J: Yes.

W: (Whew!)

A Present for Father

(Two days prior to Father's Day, June 19th, 2005.)

J: Father, do you know what I'm giving you for Father's Day?

W: No.

J: Do you want to know?

W: Sure, but only if it won't spoil a surprise.

J: No, it's OK.

W: OK.

J: Then ask me.

W: Jennifer, what are you going to give me for Father's Day?

J: I'm going to cooperate with you!

W: !!

J: All day!

And, in fact, Sunday was particularly pleasant because my five-year old lived up to her stated intention!

(Side note. Sometime between March and June of 2005, you decided to stop calling me Dadda and started calling me Father. And have since.)

12 The Concept of a Good Death

Karen, Jennifer and I are returning home. It was evening. We were heading east on Route 124 between Chester and Mendham. We had just seen the movie, *Madagascar*. A question issues forth from the car seat in back.

J: Father?

W: Yes.

J: Would you like to live for a hundred years?

W: Well, Jen, I have to give you two answers to that. One is, Yes, I'd like to be around to enjoy you and Mommy and for all of us to have each other. And the other answer is this: it is really more important to me to be in good health than to live for a very long time. If I could be reasonably healthy and die quickly, I would prefer that to living a long time with one thing and then another going wrong.

(brief silence)

J: You mean like the people in the wave?

W: ? ? You mean the tsunami?

J: Yes!

W: Yes, Jennifer. Exactly like that. Most of them died very quickly. They didn't get sick and have their bones and other things break down.

    (Karen and I look at each other. J has, it appears, got the concept of a good death. Unbelievable!)

13   First Italian Words

(I must go back for this cute one. Before I forget it. Mid-April 2004.)

We were in Italy, in Greve-in-Chianti, about 30 miles south of Florence, for Sarah's wedding to Nico, [another one, Generani, not the Paris Nick, Kramer],

(A very brief more set-up, please.) I had been trying to use to the new language you would be hearing, so I would repeat little phrases, like "please" and "thank you" of course, and some simple sentences, in Italian, like, "bring this to the table," and "let's feed the cat."

And we would listen to what I called "The Maria Tapes" which are cassettes of songs that we would listen to all the time in the car.

OK, so we were in Pescara having had dinner in a local restaurant. Grandma Marie, was with us, as was Costantino, her uncle, and his family. Costantino, I and the other gentleman had said our goodnights. Several times, as is the Italian custom. The women, however, had only said theirs two or three times and in *this* family, or perhaps in Italy generally, it is equivalent to being impolite to part without multiple rounds of (chiacchiere) chatting. And hugging, and kissing, like it was definitely the last time you were ever going to see these people.

I had tried two or three times, discretely, to pry Karen away, but, no dice. You tried to help me, but even the little voice was unable to overcome the command performance that was going on with the women.

Finally, the little one said, "Andiamo! Mamma, let's go."

That was the spell-breaker! The curtain fell on the protracted Female Parting Ceremony. That was you first Italian utterance, other than "per piacere" and "grazie."

14   You'll Be Canceled!

(Thursday, mid or late July 2005)

J: (to Father) Oh yeah, well if you don't do what I want, I'll cancel you from the Polar Bear Club!

(The Polar Bear Club was to start that Sunday, supposedly. And it was to consist of doing projects, riding horses, and other good things. ... Who knew?)

15   <u>Different Driving Styles</u>

(Approximately June 2005)

J: Father?

W: Yes….

J: Why do you get more greens than Momma?

W: What?

J: You know, more greens.

W: (?) You mean more green lights?

J: Yes!

W: Um … well … I think it's because I try harder, to get them.

J: Yes, Momma gets more yellows and reds.

16 Wherefore Babies?

(August 2005, You and I are returning home from having driven Karen to work.)

J: Father….

W: Yes….

J: Why do girls have tooties and boys have penises?

W: [Right on schedule. What is the question of most importance? Great, I get to answer this. Actually, I'm honored that she would just as soon ask me as ask her mother. [But, how much to tell an almost-six-year-old?]
Jen, you know, animals like us or horses or cats and birds, are all either female or male. With us, a female is called a woman which really means a womb-man. A "womb-man" is a person who has room inside her body to grow a baby. Maybe she should be called a "room-man" or a "room-person" because she has this space inside her body to grow a baby, and this space is called a womb. And on the outside of her body where her vagina ends is her vulva, or "tootie." That's what you see. Your tootie.

A male has a penis which can get hard temporarily and he —the man, the horse or the bird— can put it inside the female's tootie and his semen can help the woman's egg start growing a baby.

J: Oh. [silence]

[And these are the easier questions! The biological ones. How one answers the harder ones yet to come I don't know. If she even asks.]

17   Playing Teacher

(Background: Item 1. Frequently, after being in the car for five or ten minutes, Jennifer reaches a tipping point and her expressive motor is fully greased. She will then talk, jabber on and on, telling a story without apparent end; and, Item 2. Like her mother, Jennifer really loves animals. So do I, but I mean, they really love 'em.)

J: Father....

W: Yes....

J: You want to play school? You want to be a teacher or a student?

W: Sure.

J: Which one?

F: Either one. I want to be the one that you don't want to be.

J: OK, I'll be the teacher?

F: OK, what will you be teaching?

J: No, no, no, no.

F: No, what?

J: You don't even know my name! Now, sit down and be quiet, and I'll tell you my name.

W: OK, I'm sitting and I'm quiet.

J: OK. ... Hello, I'm ... Mrs. Animal-Petters.

[What a perfect name! Clearly it shows of what is her highest prior.]

18   <u>I Am Six</u>!

(October 23, 2005. We've returned from bringing Karen to work and it's time for a bath. Jennifer is getting out of her long-sleeved shirt, and I don't want the additional small chore of re-pulling out her sleeves.)

W: Up, up.

J: I know how to do it! [Not quite.]

W: Hold the wrist.

J: Father! I do not need supervision! [sic!] I am six years old! Do you think I am three years old?

Thanks, but ....

(November 18, 2005 around 9PM. Driving home from Grandma's. Karen is still there working on a dollhouse that she was constructing from a kit for Emma at Christmas.)

J: Father....

W: Yes....

J: Father, where does Santa live?

W: Jen, I believe he lives at the North Pole.

J: Oh. Is that in the sky?

W: No, it's on Earth. It's the very tip top part of the earth. It's the pole, the North Pole, (gestures).

J: But father, can reindeer fly? How would they fly with no wings? And, wouldn't his carriage I mean sleigh fall down?

W: Good thinking!

J: Thanks —but how can reindeer fly? And is it near Alaska?

W: I don't know. Maybe it's just a story.

J: No, it's not just a story! But how do they do it?

W: Jen honey, I don't know. Maybe it's just a story.

J: No. I think it's real.

W: Good.

J: I think it's real.

W: Good, enjoy it.

Men

(February 2006. At home. Out of the blue. [Refer back to The Question, August 2005]

J: Father….

W: Yes.

J: Why, did you say, men have penises??

20 Go on! It's fascinating!

(On the ride home from Marie and Franks, Grandma and Grandpa.)

J: (To Karen and me generally) Why don't we spell, "love," l-u-v?

K: (gives her answer.)

(silence)

W: Jennifer, would you like me to give an expanded answer?

J: Yes.

W: (I explain about English having two main roots, unlike most other languages. Most have one root.)

[3-way talk. I mix general ideas with concrete examples to make sure she can get it and after ten minutes, I stop.

I think that's enough for now. Did you understand it, or some of it?

J: Yes. Go on! It's fascinating!

W: !?! So, I go on. You can check this with Karen. I expand the focus and then contract it again to simple things that I know she knows the ^ tone pattern of Zao-Shang-Hao and Wan-Shang-Hao, (Chinese for "Good morning," and "Good evening") and after ten minutes again —we've driven through the Great Swamp— I stop talking.

J: No, don't stop. Keep talking about this till we get home!

W: Jen, I think this is enough. Besides, I want silence. And, I have nothing more to say.

J: (silent while debating) OK.

21 <u>A Gift for Father</u>

(Saturday, June 22, 2006, the day before Father's Day.)

J: Father.

W: Mmmh.

J: "Tomorrow you are going to have a very god day. All day!

W: Oh. Good! How do you know?

J: Because, I'm going to obey you. (smiles) All day! (laughs, snickers)

22   Languages

(This month Jen learned to ride a bicycle, without training wheels. She is so happy that she hums as she cycles. One song I heard while shadowing her on my bike, was "She'll Be Comin' Round the Mountain.")

She had learned "yes" and "no" in Chinese; "yao" and "boo yao."

She also learned "goodbye" in Polish, "doh zvidaynya," which is very like the Russian, "das vidahnya," which she already knew.

23   Italian

[Rome-Sulmona-Assisi-Rome] (During the third day in Sulmona,)

Jennifer says: "Father, I want to talk Italian," and proceeds to do so with help of course, but doing some of it on her own!

Three years of off-the-cuff teaching, cajoling, singing, reading, teasing, playing and making a fool of myself have paid off! My horse came in!

("Gentle" reader, here are some examples to vet these stories.)

A- In the gelato store,

J: Father, how do you say that again ... (gestures)?

W: Oh, you mean, to politely say, 'I want?'

J: Yes!

W: Vorrei. [pronounced, vor ray ee]

(I go to say more but she waves my forearm away, and emphatically says to la comessa, the saleswoman, Vorrei un piccolo cono di cioccolata, ... (I encourage her by gesture), ... per piacere.

"La Comessa: O, brava!" as she hands you a chocolate cone with a wafer in it, along with a big smile.

B- We had had a wonderful day with, among others, Filippo and Flavia. This vignette concerns Filippo and you. He is one of those rare people and still rarer men who bond wholeheartedly with children. Anyway, you and Filippo had an afternoon of easy bonding and silliness and you felt so comfortable with him that you fell asleep in his arms while the other eleven adults were still yacking away.)

The next evening, in the dining room of Ersilia, (the matriarch), Ersilia telephoned Flavia, one of her daughters, who lives with Filippo. "Oh, I want to talk. I want to talk with him!" says you. So, the telephone was passed to you and for five or more minutes you and he somehow conversed. Gentle reader, Filippo does not speak English and you know how much Italian Jennifer had at that point. Nevertheless, when Jennifer requested it, I gave her what help I was capable of. (Not a whole lot.) But not much help was all she needed. So, after a time — we all did not know what was being said to you—you said, "Mercoledi," (Wednesday).

We didn't know what was asked, but you followed it, and responded with the answer. The correct answer.

Wow!

The Future Epistemologist?

(February 2, 2007, Thursday, 6:30PM)

We are returning home from Madison, (NJ). You had ballet and I met Karen and you for dinner. The car ride was mellow and unusually quiet. After about ten minutes I push in a Great Courses tape cassette I've been listening to on the History of Linguistics. The lecturer is making a point about semantics, deriving his point from deSaussure's 1906 *General Theory of Linguistics* when I hear…

J: Father?

W: Yes, Jen.

J: How does he [deSaussure] know that? I mean, how does he know that's true?

[!!! She's seven.]

25 <u>Put Out Who</u>?!

(February 2007, 3AM of the night previous to the last story.)

Background: (Gentle reader, you have two know that we have two cats: "Squirt," and, according to Jennifer, "Kitten," and according to me, "Cinders." You, "gentle reader," also need to know that we had been visited for several weeks by a neighbor cat, "Inky," according to all of us.

Now, on the night in question, Jennifer was sleeping with us and, due to our schedules —Karen working weekend nights— we hardly had time to really talk, (Karen and I, that is). So, after attending to whatever it was that woke us up, we started talking. Karen and I were discussing Inky —his being an "outside" cat, his maybe having worms and so on.

As a joke, I say to Karen that we should bring in Inky, who is so cute and friendly, and put out Cinders, who is semi-feral. She allows only Jennifer to pick her up and hold her or even come near her.

Immediately, from a sleeping position, with eyes closed the whole time, we hear,

We'll put *you* out!

26   <u>Santa</u>

(December 2007, around 7PM, driving home from dropping Mom of at SBMC, Saint Barnabas Medical Center)

J: Father....

W: Yes....

J: How does he know where everyone lives?

(No intro, but I know right away who....)

W: Uh, I am not sure. Maybe he has a Global Positioning Unit.

(Silence. She's not buying it.)

J: And he's fat. So, how would he get down chimneys?

W: You know, that's a good question. I've been wondering that myself.

J: And how does he know if you've been naughty or nice?

W: He just can, Jen. I don't know.

Generosity

(December 2007) Background:

a- Grandpa doesn't like cats. And Grandma and he wanted a dog, if anything. And, it must be an Irish setter. They've had two. [And they didn't train them and they, those dogs, need a farm to live on and not a house to live in. And both Grands are older now and couldn't manage a high-strung strong dog.]

b-Karen had said Yes to a cat rescue group two years ago. We got a call one night and just as I said No to the inquiry, Karen walked in the door and asked, "Who is it?" ... And so, long story short, we fostered the pregnant homeless cat, later named, Willow.)

Story: Jennifer saw the birth and learned much about biology and also about all the forethought that Karen had given to keeping out two cats separate from Willow and her kittens.

Six months later, (this started around March of '07), we found a great home for two of the kittens, a male and a female who looked alike in their tabby stripes. And, the woman who took them took them both so they could stay together. Some cats have all the luck.

Anyway, the last kitten, a dark grey with yellow eyes, was named Wolfie. Jennifer was subduing him, meaning, besides handling and gentling him, she would carry him everywhere and pet him and talk with him. He was subdued. He purred almost all the time. If you looked at him, he purred. If anybody picked him up, he purred. Naturally, this made everyone feel good.

We brought Wolfie over to Granma and Grandpa's a few times. Naturally, they fell in love with him. Even Grandpa.

Christmas was coming. They made a few gentle, tentative inquiries to see if Jennifer would feel OK about letting Wolfie stay with them.

J: You mean live with you?

Gma: Yes.

J: No!

Gma: I understand. Of course.

Within about a month, without prompting, Jennifer let them have Wolfie, with the understanding that

J: When I come to over, I'm still his cat-mother.

Gma and Gpa: OK, it's a deal. (Big smiles.)

28   Intuitive Economics

(August 28th, 2008, Thursday night during the acceptance speech of Barak Obama.)

J: How? How will he do that?

W: That's a great question!

J: I mean, how does he get the money, to do those things.

(Out of the mouth of babes.)

W: Jen, it's complicated. I'll talk with you later. Let's listen for now.

Emotional Fact-checking

It was another long, fun-filled day. You didn't want to go to bed (All kids get cranky when they're tired, and for that matter, so do adults.) You were giving Mom a hard time. She was tired and cranky too and was in bed already.

Background: About three weeks earlier you had asked me, in the characteristic way you often began important questions…

J: Father?

W: Yes….

J: When you were young, did you want to grow up?

W: Yes…. Is that what you mean to ask?

J: Well, not exactly. I mean, I want to grow up in some ways but in some ways I don't!

W: Oh, Sweetie, of course. It's great to look forward to growing up and being able to do the things you want, but it's also great to be a kid and sad to leave behind all those things.

So, you and Mom were starting to go at it, a bit. Usually, I would intervene to support her but this time I didn't, both because I didn't want to and because I knew that you and she would play the three-way dynamic against me. So, the back-and-forth went on for a bit and then Mom got stern and you decided to cooperate. Well, more precisely, you decided to try to overcome your fear. Fear? Of what?

Ghosts. Who live in closets.

Now, I respected that you were nine-and-three-quarters years old, not three! or even six, and I know you know Scoobie-Doo and things like that are make believe, so what is this nonsense about being afraid of ghosts in closets? And also, you advised us, in basements,.

Anyway, you went into your room and laid down, and stayed there. After about five minutes I decided to go in, to comfort you. (I knew, or suspected, that you didn't need it and I felt I had given enough time for Mom to establish what she wanted with you.) I lay there just a few minutes and you said,

J: Father.

W: Mmmhmmm.

J: Why did you come in?

W: ...Love...

[Not another word was spoken or needed.]

30   The Downside of Human Nature

(July 24th, 2009)

J: Father?

W: ...Daughter?

J: Why did the people who came here kill the Indians?

W: Oh, Jen, that is complicated.

J: I know, but why'd they have to kill them off?

W: OK, OK. I'll give you an answer, later. I need time to think about how to organize my answer. And, you must finish your math drill.

(And about four hours later, we did have a discussion that lasted a half-hour. Then you needed and took a nap.)

Yeah, Sure….

(Approximately Spring 2009. Background: three years ago, I bought a Vespa motorscooter. An ET-4, 150, lime green. I had given you rides on it with you sitting in back and in front to get you used to it and to teach you how it handles and how to control it. In an elementary way, I taught you what I could about the parts and a little about the insides.)

J: (in a particularly innocent and bright tone) Father?

W: Yes.

J: You showed me everything about "Minty" (our nickname for my motorscooter) except how to start it.

W: (almost guffawing!) Well, Jennifer, when I started teaching you about it, I had to make a decision. I wanted you to know about it so you could handle it, eventually, and maybe even care for it somewhat, but I did not want you to know how to start it.

J: (smiling and in a reassuring voice) I'd never start it or take it.

W: Oh Jen, I just don't want that to be a possibility. Certainly not before you are allowed to operate it legally.

J: But I wouldn't take it.

W: Jen, let's say you wouldn't take it for a ride. Just starting it and getting it off its stand is beyond you. It's heavy and you can't control it, weight-wise, yet.

J: But I just want to know how to start it.

W: Jen, I'm not going to teach you that yet.

J: But….

W: "Stop. If you're so fired up to learn how … there's a manual downstairs in the basement. If you can find it, and if you can read it and understand it, then you can teach yourself how to start the scooter.

[I should mention that the manual is in Italian.]

The Cat Who Converses

(April 2011) This story is not about you; it's about Squirt, our Siamese, who I nicknamed, and we all agree is, The Smartest Cat in America.

I was sitting on the top step of the stairs putting on my sneakers to take Wolfie [the dog this time, not the previous kitten of the same name; the dog really does look something like a wolf]. Squirt snuck by my right elbow and the partially closed garage door. He walked halfway through the garage —the door was already now opened—when I said, "Squirt!" with my tone saying, "What do you think you're doing?"

He stops. He does *not* turn around, and issues a defiant, "Rearowww!" with his tone telling me he's going out and he continues walking. Tail up.

(This is merely one example. Oh, I could tell you of the times Mom or I came home and found the glass kibble jar either turned over or opened. Yes, in fact, opened! Unscrewed. The first few times I said, "OK, the dog threw a party". But no, Jose, no way, because one day we saw him, Squirt, nudging the glass jar toward the basement stairs tapping it to knock it down, knowing, I swear, that the metal cap might be dislodged if it rolled and bounced down the stairs!

And then there was the time when we caught him, right in front of us, fiddling with the cap with his front paws! That must have been how the jar was opened when they threw the parties. He figured out how to put uneven pressure on the cap to loosen it. It wasn't the dog. Squirt was much more intelligent and resourceful than the dog.)

33 He's Just a Psychologist!

So, we were in the car (about six months ago, say, February 2011): you me and Lily. Relevant fact for later, Lily's mother is Philippine. I had left you two alone but, after a while, so as not to feel only as the chauffeur, I decide to try my hand at interacting with Lily, and you.

(Now, you know much of the background and you know the rest of the story, but I have to write it up because all of the diverse pieces are essential, and my "gentle readers" could not understand it without this background.)

First, you know my intense interest if languages and cultures. You yourself can recognize —not speak, but recognize— many languages now, and you can also good-guess where the speaker comes from.

And, you know how to greet people in many languages including Tagalog, the language of the Philippines —you sense where this is going?— Chinese, Korean, as well as the "usual suspects," Italian, Spanish, French and German.

So, to focus the background more, you have to remember that I had greeted Lily's mother, Jocelyn, in Tagalog, "Magandan oomaga." She was so flabbergasted that she could not quite speak. She looked at me quizzically, not quite processing it. When she gathered herself and haltingly said something back, I pursued with something more, (you know ... "Ka mustaka.," and was ready to hear, "Booty," and reply, "Ma Booty.")

With big eyes she says, "How you know?!"

With both my most modest face on and my hands signaling, I say, "I can't really talk about it," but before she defers to me —which is what I *don't* want— and shifts her attention, so I say confidentially and softly, "I did some work for the government."

"Oh!" she says co-conspiratorially, and nods. Then gaining her courage and to show me she's knowledgeable, she asks, "CIA?" I look around, needlessly cautious, body language indicating that I must make sure no one is overhearing us, and nod imperceptibly and modestly.

Now, you saw all this, and later asked me, Why?

J: And, what would you have said if she pressed for more?

W: I told you, because everybody loves a good story. And it was harmless. No harm could come from it.

I saw you internally debate what I said and waited until you absorbed that.

Then I told you that, if necessary, I would have mentioned, *very* confidentially, having been on Mindanao and helping with the Abu Musaef problem. I didn't have to, but I was prepared. (The CIA calls this going down to the third level. I was never in the Central Intelligence Agency, by the way, gentle reader, nor did I help take down the Abu Musaef terrorist group. But Jocelyn, Lily's mother, would have known distinctly and fearfully all about that. She would have been convinced, and known *not* to ask further questions. I would not have had to say more. These *are* dangerous matters. You never know.)

You also asked me the same question, Why? about the Sikhs —the gas station guys who wear turbans— and I told you that they were astonished and very happy to be greeted in their language ("Sata sri agal"), and if they asked —which two did— I would have off-handedly mentioned having living briefly in

Srinigar, India. They were very happy to share that tiny fragment of experience with me. (Invented fragment.) It didn't matter that I knew, and you knew, it was make believe. (Had they asked more, I would have told them something particular about a mosque near a bakery. I didn't have to, but I was ready. Every place has a bakery and there are many mosques, all over the place. One would surely have been near a bakery. Sikhs don't go to mosque, but they live near Moslems. I was ready.)

So, (with all that as sufficient background...), I turn to Lily and ask, "Say, Lily, if I said, 'Magandan Oomaga' to you, would you understand what I said?"

The words are not out of my mouth —even *before* I complete saying them— you say, "Oh, *no! There* he goes!" You raise your voice and abruptly say, "**Don't pay any attention to him**!" You become more excited and gesticulate "*Not*" signs to Lily, and try to distract her. No attention should be paid to me!

Lily's face shows several emotions: "What did he say?" and, "Why is Jennifer so energized?" and, "What's going on here?" and "I've never seen Jennifer like this" and "I don't understand what's going on here."

[The fun has started. I know I have you now, and I might have her too.]

So, I start to talk but only a word or two gets out because you interrupt me, intercepting my attempt to see where things will go with Lily. Lily looks at you, then looks at me. I have put on my innocent, parental, concerned, ready-to-explain face, "I'm slightly confused, myself."

I open my mouth. I'm not really going to speak because I know you're not going to let me —but Lily doesn't know this— and you start singing, loudly, then humming, and making blare-out-loud nonsense sounds so that Lily doesn't get sucked into this movie of mine.

Lily looks like:

'Huh? I don't know what's going on. Is this good or bad? And Jennifer is usually so balanced, but this is really different. Also, something interesting is going on here, between them, and I don't have a clue.'

So, I let this *mise-en-scene* —this little drama— go on until you take a breath and then I strike! I start to say something, anything, maybe even something reassuring to Lily, when you start! You wave your hands energetically. You talk loudly to override anything I might have been going to say.

You almost yell, "He's just a psychologist!" [meaning: He's **not** Indiana Jones! He's *not* CIA. Don't believe *any* story he is going to tell you!] which just confuses Lily more.

Lily can't possibly understand what is embedded in your statement —what you mean by "He's just a psychologist!"— and to lower the boil, you say, "But, he's got his facts straight" [meaning: that if she asks me something, if she says *anything*, she will get sucked into my movie. I will respond with something which captures her imagination and further engages her in a 'movie.' It will be entertaining, make sense, be plausible, even factual —I've got my facts straight— and fun, but it will entangle her in an engrossing story. She might or might not fully understand it or believe exactly, but she would enjoy it; it would be plausible.

You don't want her to believe *a thing* about *anything* I might say. You know it's all just a "movie." Just a story, and she shouldn't be taken in.

(At twelve-and-a-half kids should be purists.)

Finally, the mood in the car changes. Lily's face looks like, "I don't get it, but no harm done."

You, Jen, look like, "Oh I hope this is *over* and you're *not going to start up* again!" "What a *hoot!*" I think, "Boy, was Jennifer energized!"

[I love it: "He's just a psychologist. ... But, he's got his facts straight."]

34   A Good Question (March 2013)
and An Answer (April 2013)

You know that I'm a psychologist and that I "do psychotherapy." You've been in my waiting room or waiting area occasionally over the years and I've introduced you to several of my patients.

You say, "Father," and I know just from your tone that a doozie of a question is coming. "How do you know what to say to them? Your patients?"

Okay...! I chuckle, and say, "Jen, I can't give you an answer to that right now. We don't have time. Let me think about it. It's very complicated.

(You know that I will get back to you on it, and I want to, because that's how I am with you. But how do I compress all that I could say, should say, into few enough words to be tolerable to listen to? I must make this a snack; more than a bite-sized nugget and less than a full dinner entrée.

So I think about it, for about two months, and you leave me in peace about it. And, actually, I am writing this up months later.

So, I ask myself, how would you define what you do? In as few words as possible, what is the essence of what a psychotherapist does?

I remind you of your question and ask if you'd like an answer now.

You: "Sure."

Well, psychotherapy is an honest conversation between a person seeking help and a person offering to help.

(I don't mention that it took time to boil down many factors to those thirteen words.)

I stop. To see what lands. You say, "Seeking help for what, and how do you know what to say to offer help?"

The conversation went on from there.

35   <u>Mom's Dream</u>; <u>Jennifer's Baby</u>

You and Mom were sleeping a few hours ago, and I rested my hand on Mom's neck and shoulder. She said, "Oh, I love the feel of you," and she moved a tad closer.

Still more asleep than not, she said, "I had a dream. Jennifer had a baby and you and the baby took a nap ... and that's how you passed. ... I hope that's how it is for you."

You know, I debated including this in this book but decided to because it says so much about the three of us: Mom, and me, our relationship —how and why we love each other even though we are so different; and you and me and our relationship—which puts such a high value on honest communication and independence. The simple fact of life and death can be talked about. (I've quoted Aristotle to you, —you know, 'Uncle Aristotle,'— "Everything has a beginning, a middle and an end," so why not include Mom's loving dream in a book of memories about you. And, she sent me off with me knowing that you had a baby, and that we were together, and that you trusted us to take a nap together. It's such a beautiful dream it chokes me up.)

By the way —I am giving in to my flow of associations— I'm not afraid of death. Pain? Infirmity? They're another story.

But I have a contingency plan (and that you must share with nobody. Mom also knows it so what I mean is, you can feel free to discuss it with her if it ever comes up. Our code for it is Huck Finn's last words, 'Guess there's nothin' left to do but head out to the Indian Territories.")

A further thought. It is what meaning we put into life that is the meaning of life.

36   <u>What Can I Leave Her</u>?

(10 AM, same day. You two are still sleeping.) You know, some years ago, probably starting when Mom was carrying you and definitely within your first few years (I, being only eight-seven at the time or something like that, I forget, [that's a joke]), asked myself, "What can I leave her?" What can I bequeath her? Money? No. The house, probably, once the mortgage is paid off. My practice? No; it's not really possible to transfer relationships and history, and besides, monetarily it's not worth much. And besides, I don't want you to become a psychologist or psychotherapist in today's world governed by Managed Care. If you wish to become a neuropsychologist that would be just fine with me.

So what can I give this creature, this girl? After some meditation I thought, I can instill a love of music, of languages and of literature. I can get her to see how being fair is possibly the highest value that a person and for that matter, a society, can achieve. I can try to help her be a balanced personality. And maybe, I can get her to love and see the value of absurdity and humor; to create and withstand the delicious simultaneous conflict between the serious, the tragic and the absurd.

I think you have it or are on track to have it. I know you love music and singing, for sure. And I know you enjoy languages, especially Italian, for sure. And you love to read. And now, thanks to Ms. Dubek, you like math and are not intimidated by it and you love science, And, you have a sense of humor and are trying to develop it. And you know a little Wing Chun and Tai Chi Chuan and how to use them. And, ballet.

And many kids love you, Ms. Animal-Petters, as do their parents and their animals. Wow. I say, this is a balanced personality. And, you are kind.

Signing off....

37   Holy Smoke! What questions!

J: Father ... ? How did you decide to become a psychologist? Did you always know you wanted to become one?

(Long pause.)

W: Okay, Jen. I have to give you two answers. You know that in life there are things that cannot be explained with just one thought.... So, yes, on one level, of all the courses I took, the ones that grabbed me the most, I mean emotionally and intellectually, were the psych classes. I felt intuitively and effortlessly related to them. (Pause.) And, of course, it was a "noble" profession, helping people.

[I stop. You say nothing. Okay. I think, Is she going to ask the follow-up question? I wait. You wait, (like a good psychologist). You let the silence do some of the work. I continue.]

W: And on the second level, when I was a child, I consciously thought —in these exact words— 'These people are crazy! They can't believe what they say and do. With no recognition! But they do. AND THEY WANT ME TO BE LIKE THEM!' "They," in this case were my parents, both, in different ways, and their reference group. (Not every member of that group, of course). When I was older, I thought more generally about these things and society at large too, so, when I came across Freud and others, and found out that there was a field that studied people at the core level, and that I could get paid for figuring them out and helping them be more "normal," and in many cases less narrow-minded and less dogmatic, more balanced —it was a natural! A slam-dunk fit.

[The question has been answered satisfactorily, but still there is an air of incompleteness. This time the silence cannot do the heavy lifting, so you say, "I thought you also considered becoming a writer. How did you decide which?"]

You ask good questions! Okay, so I say what in one or two sentences what took a few years to boil down.
W: Jen, I intuitively knew I would be a great psychologist. Without doubt. But a writer? That's a much more chancy thing. There is no way of knowing how you will earn money. And, besides, I felt I had in me one great novel, but beyond that, I didn't know.

[So, I think the question has been answered and you are well nourished with answers. But No, your imagination has been piqued and you ask the follow-up question.]

J: What would your novel have been about?

[!!!] (Oh, no.)

W: Love, death, falling in love, and when if ever is murder justified?

[Silence. Finally, you have had enough. That's it for this conversation. The inquirer has drilled down enough and needs to contemplate. She has no further questions, your honor.]

The Cougar Dream

(Early September 2013, on vacation, in Vermont)

I have a dream. I see a crow; it becomes a hawk. I become the hawk. I'm gliding around and over a rise. I see a bunch of children hurrying up the hill. You are lagging behind.

I see a cougar. It sees you. You have a cellophane bag with kibbles in it. You toss some of them between you and the cougar. You go closer, not hurriedly, but I know that you're wishing to get closer to the elegant, powerful pussycat.

You look at him. He looks at you.

I see in his eyes the thought, "Her! Lunch! Kibbles later."

I wake up.

39   Ba Duan Jen

(September 17, 2014) Gentle reader, Ba Duan J*in*, is an eight-step exercise sequence that both Jen and I had studied. The title of the poem is a play on those Chinese words. "Ba," by the way, gentle reader, means eight. J*in* / Jen.

Birthday card:

> She's balanced as a spider on eight legs.
> She's supple as an octopus, mentally.
> Cute, smart, loving and kind —
>> What is this? A love poem?
>> Who is it to?
>>> Yes it is,
>>>> and Happy 15th birthday, Jen.
>
> Love,
> Father

Haiku

(For your 16th birthday)

The Universe, Dig it!

The universe. Death.

The death of the universe.

Dao, Wuxi, Taiji.

Dig it.

Yin and Yang.

Gravity, entropy.

Embrace the mystery.

(Btw, that is a double haiku. But who's counting?)

(September 18th, 2015) You insist on a correction! You are right. Seventeen sounds. And they must be a 5-7-5 pattern. So, ...

The universe. Death.

The death of the universe.

Dao, Wuxi, Taiji.

Dig it, yin with yang.

So embrace the mystery.

Grav'ty, entropy.

41   Another "Me Do!" Story

(You were 2 to 2-and-a-half years old. Already independent. So much so that I nicknamed you with your own often said words, "Me Do!")

You were at the top of the stairs, with Mom. I was at the bottom putting on my sneakers.

You wanted to go down by yourself. So you took a step, (you must have pushed away Mom's hand —I didn't see it. You started to tumble. Mom screamed! William!

You know how things go in slow motion in an emergency? The top step is thirteen. So in your first tumble your arm and hand are up. You are at step ten, but still tumbling. I'm sitting on two. From playing stickball and punchball as a kid, I know instantly that I can't reach you immediately no matter how fast I tried, and I know that and on your next turn you will be foot-side down but still tumbling. I delay a half-second purposely then thrust out my hands to cup your neck and head, and then draw you to me taking in some of your momentum.

It would have been bad if you had impacted. Okay. Smile. No hurt. No damage.

Reassure Karen. Relief.

You? No problem.

"Me-Do!"

42   Why Aren't My Half-Brothers in My Life?

(August 11, 2019. Jen, now you are nineteen, twenty next month. I haven't written anything lately and this will probably be the last entry in your book, or should I say, my memory book of your most memorable moments. So, here we go.)

You have always asked great questions, such as, "How does he know that?" and, "Why do men have penises??? Well, you came out with another great one: "Have you changed?"

You asked me that first when you were sixteen. You were going through a hard period of wanting more family and you were trying to understand why your half-brothers —that's the designation they would give, rather than the open-hearted "brothers" that you feel and wish to feel— do not have contact with you, or me, or Mom. I answered you then; fully. But it is important enough to do so again, here on paper, now, because you may wish to reach out again —if I know you— and I want to minimize the pain you will feel.

But back to you, before I enlarge the backstory. You must have been thinking about how they, especially Andrew, could not want to know you, and me, and all of us. Right?

To deduce your question you must have been a lot of psychological detective work, (technically, projective-identification). Maybe I had changed. And drastically, because you have known me to be the way I have been with you for your whole life, consistently for almost two decades.

I had answered you completely honestly then, as I always have.

W: No. I have not changed. I had been with Kenneth and Andrew as I have been with you. I've always been visible as a person and not hidden behind a role, and I've been comfortable with the different sides that being a father means. One small example: just as I have with you, I recited poems to Andrew to help him go to sleep while I did yoga on the floor beside his bed.

So, Why? you must be asking. There is a short and coherent answer which I will repeat momentarily. The long answer is very, very, very long and is mired in acrimony and contrasting worldviews and is, in large part, none of your business —which I say most respectfully— but there are some things that the generations need to keep separate.

As the judge said to Andrew when his mother and I were in court, yet again, "I don't like to litigate parental disputes in front of the children. So would you [Andrew], please remove yourself from the courtroom." Andrew ,who was himself a new lawyer, demurred. The judge told him to leave. He left, of course.

After losing motion after motion, I won that one; the judge officially emancipated Andrew, which means that I no longer had to pay her for him, even after college which is what she wanted!

In very brief, the larger story is this. I was a good father, maybe a very good one. Andrew's mom, like yours, was an excellent mother. He loved her. Whatever he felt for me, and I do believe he loved me too, it was his intense love for her, plus, he knew that I was glad for him loving her and even siding with her up to a point, slightly, maybe. But, he knew that she would have gone absolutely, bat-shit-crazy angry, and would have played the *devastated-without-end* card if he had contact with you, me, or us.

He had seen how she could sustain anger for years. She was not an angry person, but the very long story is very deep and none of anybody else's business, so I'll leave it at that. In short, if it meant devastating her, enduringly, perhaps even to the point that she would uncomfortable with him, and his wife, and his children eventually, versus losing me and mine, the decision was clear.

My view? It is tragic. It is sad —needlessly so, and so sad for you, and us—but an atomic bomb would have been detonated both in her mind and in his life. The Japanese do not give up. The Emperor of Japan ended World War II to spare his population further nuking. He felt that his remaining people should not endure more Hiroshimas and Nagasakis. He had to think of his people!

But the wide view is —although from our angle cowardly on Andrew's part— in the long run it was the right choice. Spare a parent *and* prevent an **unending** nuclear war even if that means tossing away another parent and all the good things he has to offer which includes a relationship with you? Some choice.

But sometimes you must choose the lesser evil. It would have been unending. I can attest to that.

Be at peace.

www.ingramcontent.com/pod-product-compliance
Lightning Source LLC
Chambersburg PA
CBHW021848090426
42811CB00033B/2176/J